Level 3: 750 vocabulary words

Four Ancient Beauties: Yang Guifei

四大美女之杨贵妃

章辉辉 改编
郭 辉 翻译

MP3 Download Online
www.sinolingua.com.cn

First Edition   2017

ISBN 978-7-5138-1324-2
Copyright 2017 by Sinolingua Co., Ltd
Published by Sinolingua Co., Ltd
24 Baiwanzhuang Road, Beijing 100037, China
Tel: (86) 10-68320585   68997826
Fax: (86) 10-68997826   68326333
http://www.sinolingua.com.cn
E-mail: hyjx@sinolingua.com.cn
Facebook: www.facebook.com/sinolingua
Printed by Beijing Jinghua Hucais Printing Co., Ltd

Printed in the People's Republic of China

编者的话

对于广大汉语学习者来说，要想快速提高汉语水平，扩大阅读量是很有必要的。"彩虹桥"汉语分级读物为汉语学习者提供了一系列有趣、有用的汉语阅读材料。本系列读物按照词汇量进行分级，力求用限定的词汇讲述精彩的故事。本套读物主要有以下特点：

一、分级精准，循序渐进。我们参考"新汉语水平考试（HSK）词汇表"（2012年修订版）、《汉语国际教育用音节汉字词汇等级划分（国家标准）》和《常用汉语1500高频词语表》等词汇分级标准，结合《欧洲语言教学与评估框架性共同标准》（CEFR），设计了一套适合汉语学习者的"彩虹桥"词汇分级标准。本系列读物分为7个级别（入门级*、1级、2级、3级、4级、5级、6级），供不同水平的汉语学习者选择，每个级别故事的生词数量不超过本级别对应词汇量的20%。随着级别的升高，故事的篇幅逐渐加长。本系列读物与HSK、CEFR的对应级别，各级词汇量以及每本书的字数详见下表。

---

* 入门级（Starter）在封底用S标识。

级别	入门级	1级	2级	3级	4级	5级	6级
对应级别	HSK1 CEFR A1	HSK1-2 CEFR A1-A2	HSK2-3 CEFR A2-B1	HSK3 CEFR A2-B1	HSK3-4 CEFR B1	HSK4 CEFR B1-B2	HSK5 CEFR B2-C1
词汇量	150	300	500	750	1 000	1 500	2 500
字数	1 000	2 500	5 000	7 500	10 000	15 000	25 000

二、**故事精彩，题材多样**。本套读物选材的标准就是"精彩"，所选的故事要么曲折离奇，要么感人至深，对读者构成奇妙的吸引力。选题广泛取材于中国的神话传说、民间故事、文学名著、名人传记和历史故事等，让汉语学习者在阅读中潜移默化地了解中国的文化和历史。

三、**结构合理，实用性强**。"彩虹桥"系列读物的每一本书中，除了中文故事正文之外，都配有主要人物的中英文介绍、生词英文注释及例句、故事正文的英文翻译、练习题和生词表，方便读者阅读和理解故事内容，提升汉语阅读能力。练习题主要采用客观题，题型多样，难度适中，并附有参考答案，既可供汉语教师在课堂上教学使用，又可供汉语学习者进行自我水平检测。

如果您对本系列读物有什么想法，比如推荐精彩故事、提出改进意见等，请发邮件到 liuxiaolin@sinolingua.com.cn，与我们交流探讨。也可以关注我们的微信公众号 CHQRainbowBridge，随时与我们交流互动。同时，微信公众号会不定期发布有关"彩虹桥"的出版信息，以及汉语阅读、中国文化小知识等。

韩　颖　刘小琳

Preface

For students who study Chinese as a foreign language, it's crucial for them to enlarge the scope of their reading to improve their comprehension skills. The "Rainbow Bridge" Graded Chinese Reader series is designed to provide a collection of interesting and useful Chinese reading materials. This series grades each volume by its vocabulary level and brings the learners into every scene through vivid storytelling. The series has the following features:

I. A gradual approach by grading the volumes based on vocabulary levels. We have consulted the New HSK Vocabulary (2012 Revised Edition), the *Graded Chinese Syllables, Characters and Words for the Application of Teaching Chinese to the Speakers of Other Languages (National Standard)* and the 1,500 Commonly Used High Frequency Chinese Vocabulary, along with the Common European Framework of Reference for Languages (CEFR) to design the "Rainbow Bridge" vocabulary grading standard. The series is divided into seven levels (Starter*, Level 1, Level 2, Level 3, Level 4, Level 5 and Level 6) for students at different stages in their Chinese education to choose from. For each level, new words are no more than 20% of the vocabulary amount as specified in the corresponding HSK and CEFR levels. As the levels progress, the passage length will in turn increase. The following table indicates the corresponding "Rainbow Bridge" level, HSK and CEFR levels, the vocabulary amount, and number of characters.

---

* Represented by "S" on the back cover.

Level	Starter	1	2	3	4	5	6
HSK/ CEFR Level	HSK1 CEFR A1	HSK1-2 CEFR A1-A2	HSK2-3 CEFR A2-B1	HSK3 CEFR A2-B1	HSK3-4 CEFR B1	HSK4 CEFR B1-B2	HSK5 CEFR B2-C1
Vocabulary	150	300	500	750	1,000	1,500	2,500
Characters	1,000	2,500	5,000	7,500	10,000	15,000	25,000

II. Intriguing stories on various themes. The series features engaging stories known for their twists and turns as well as deeply touching plots. The readers will find it a joyful experience to read the stories. The topics are selected from Chinese mythology, legends, folklore, literary classics, biographies of renowned people and historical tales. Such wide-ranging topics exert an invisible, yet formative, influence on readers' understanding of Chinese culture and history.

III. Reasonably structured and easy to use. For each volume of the "Rainbow Bridge" series, apart from a Chinese story, we also provide an introduction to the main characters in Chinese and English, new words with English explanations and sample sentences, and an English translation of the story, followed by comprehension exercises and a vocabulary list to help users read and understand the story and improve their Chinese reading skills. The exercises are mainly presented as objective questions that take on various forms with moderate difficulty. Moreover, keys to the exercises are also provided. The series can be used by teachers in class or by students for self-study.

If you have any questions, comments or suggestions about the series, please email us at liuxiaolin@sinolingua.com.cn. You can also exchange ideas with us via our WeChat account: CHQRainbowBridge. This account will provide updates on the series along with Chinese reading materials and cultural tips.

Han Ying and Liu Xiaolin

主要人物和地点
Main Characters and Places

李隆基（Lǐ Lóngjī）：唐朝在位最久的皇帝。在他统治期间，唐朝进入全盛时期，史称"开元盛世"。后来"安史之乱"发生，唐朝走向衰落。

Li Longji: The longest reigning emperor of the Tang Dynasty (618-907). Tang reached its pinnacle of development during his reign, which was known as the Kaiyuan Era. Late in his reign, the An-Shi Rebellion occurred, marking the beginning of Tang's decline.

杨玉环（Yáng Yùhuán）：李隆基的妃子，是中国古代四大美女之一。

Yang Yuhuan: Beloved concubine of Li Longji, one of the four great beauties in ancient China

高力士（Gāo Lìshì）：李隆基身边的太监，最懂得李隆基的心思，帮李隆基做了很多事情。

Gao Lishi: One of the eunuchs and the closest confidant of Li Longji. He assisted Li Longji in a great number of affairs.

杨国忠（Yáng Guózhōng）：杨贵妃的哥哥。

Yang Guozhong: Yang Yuhuan's elder brother

李瑁（Lǐ Mào）：李隆基的儿子，杨玉环的前夫。

Li Mao: Son of Li Longji, ex-husband of Yang Yuhuan

长安（Cháng'ān）：中国唐代的首都，就是现在的西安。

Chang'an: The capital of the Tang Dynasty, which was located in present-day Xi'an

马嵬坡（Mǎwéipō）：又名马嵬驿，位于今陕西省兴平市。

Mawei Po: An area situated in present-day Xingping City, Shaanxi Province

四川（Sìchuān）：位于中国西南方向的一个省。
Sichuan: A province in southwestern China

蓬莱岛（Pénglái Dǎo）：汉族神话传说中的海上神山，为神仙居住的地方。

Penglai Island: A legendary mountain in the sea in Chinese mythology where the immortals live

月宫（Yuègōng）：中国古代神话传说中月亮上的宫殿。
Moon Palace: A legendary palace on the moon in ancient Chinese mythology

中文故事

四大美女之杨贵妃

一、李隆基初遇杨玉环

一千多年以前，中国唐朝①有个皇帝②叫李隆基。李隆基做了好几十年的皇帝，是一个非常成功的皇帝。

李隆基五十多岁的时候，他最喜欢的妃子③病死了，他很伤心④。失去最喜欢的妃子，李隆基经常心情不好，太监⑤高力士就想

① 唐朝（Tángcháo）
n. Tang Dynasty
e.g., 杨贵妃是唐朝人。

② 皇帝（huángdì）*n.* emperor
e.g., 皇帝想做什么都可以。

③ 妃子（fēizi）*n.* concubine
e.g., 皇帝可以有很多妃子。

④ 伤心（shāngxīn）*adj.* sad
e.g., 她最好的朋友走了，她很伤心。

⑤ 太监（tàijiàn）*n.* eunuch
e.g., 太监是伺候皇帝的人。

办法让他高兴。

这天天气很好，皇宫①花园里的花都开了。高力士知道皇帝很喜欢看花，就对李隆基说："皇上，我们去花园那边看看花吧！"李隆基说："好啊，现在花很好看，我们去看看吧。"

有个女人正在花园里休息，她看到两个男人向这边走来，有点不好意思，就拿了一朵花，挡②住了自己一半的脸，向另一个方向走了。

李隆基看到了这个女人，他发现这个女人真的是太漂亮了。虽然她拿着花挡住了一半脸，但是她的脸比花还要好看。高力士也觉得自己从来没见过

① 皇宫（huánggōng）
n. imperial palace
e.g., 故宫是中国古代的皇宫。

② 挡（dǎng）*v.* hide
e.g., 你不要挡住我的视线。

这么好看的女人。这时这个女人回头看了一下,看到了正在看她的<u>李隆基</u>,就笑了一下,然后才慢慢地走了。她这一回头,<u>李隆基</u>心里十分高兴,他觉得这个女人应该也很喜欢他。<u>李隆基</u>站在那里看着这个女人走远,一直到再也看不见。

二、李隆基设法娶玉环

高力士是最懂李隆基的人，他能很快知道李隆基在想什么，他也能知道李隆基想去做什么。他能提前做好李隆基想做的事情，所以李隆基喜欢高力士在自己身边。

高力士很快就知道了在花园和皇帝见面的女人是李隆基的儿子李瑁的王妃①杨玉环。他想，怎么会这样呢？世界上有这么多的女人，皇帝喜欢谁不行，却喜欢上自己儿子的王妃，这真的是不好办！要是其他的人知道了，他们会觉得皇帝不该这样做……高力士是最懂李隆基的人，他知道皇帝好不容易才找

① 王妃（wángfēi）n. wife of a prince
e.g., 很多人都喜欢戴安娜王妃。

① 同时（tóngshí）
conj. moreover, in addition
e.g., 她是我的同学，同时也是我最好的朋友。

② 真相（zhēnxiàng）
n. truth
e.g., 真相只有一个。

③ 果然（guǒrán）
adv. as expected
e.g., 他果然知道谁是班长。

到喜欢的女人，所以一定要想出一个解决的好办法：既能让皇帝和杨玉环在一起，同时①又不让别人知道事情的真相②。

高力士想了好几天，终于想出了一个好办法。他马上去见皇帝，说："皇上还记得我们在花园见到的那个女人吧？"李隆基听到高力士说起这个女人，他很高兴，心想，果然③高力士是最懂我的人，知道我在想什么，看来他已经找到了那个女人。于是李隆基就说："你找到那个女人了吗？我觉得这个女人很漂亮，我很喜欢。"高力士回答说："是的，我找到那个女人了。那个女人叫

杨玉环,是您的儿子李瑁王爷①的王妃。"

李隆基听了高力士的话,很不高兴。他想:那个女人怎么是李瑁的王妃?如果这样的话,我就不能和她在一起了。

高力士看到李隆基很不高兴,于是赶快说:"虽然杨玉环现在是王妃,但她以后可以不是王妃,那

① 王爷(wángye)
n. prince, His Highness
e.g., 这个公园以前是清朝的一个王爷的。

① 解决（jiějué）v.
resolve
e.g., 你来解决这个问题。

② 祈福（qífú）v.
pray for blessings
e.g., 我在为母亲祈福。

③ 道观（dàoguàn）n. Taoist temple
e.g., 道观里很安静。

④ 出家（chūjiā）v.
become a monk or nun
e.g., 他出家当了和尚。

时您就可以跟她在一起了。"李隆基听说有解决①的办法，就说："怎么让她不是李瑁的王妃？说来听听。"

高力士说："您就说要为您的母亲祈福②，需要一个女人去道观③出家④，然后您就让李瑁的王妃离开这里，去道观。这样杨玉环就不是李瑁王爷的王妃了。"

李隆基听了之后，觉得并不是什么好办法，就说："这是什么办法啊？她去了道观，以后我也不能见她了啊？我觉得这样不行。"

高力士看到皇帝不同意，又说："杨玉环去了道观之后，不再用她以前的名字，我们给她一个新的名字，这样大家看到的是一个不认识的人，就没有人知道她原来是王妃了，时间一长大家都忘了，然后您再去道观把她接①回来，这样就可以了。"

李隆基听完了之后点点头，说："这样做，我看行，高力士你真聪明啊！但是我觉得，李瑁应该心里不高兴，有可能不同意，所以我再给他找个王妃吧。"

高力士说："好的，我先去找李瑁王爷，让他知道这个事情，然后让他来见您。"

李瑁听高力士说皇帝让自己的王妃去道观祈福，然后他可以得到一个新的王妃，他很不高兴，不愿意这样做。但是因为这是

① 接（jiē）v. pick up, meet
e.g., 别忘了下班后去接孩子。

① 命令（mìnglìng）
n. command, order
e.g., 你敢不听我的命令？

② 违抗（wéikàng）v.
disobey
e.g., 他公开违抗父母，一个人出国了。

③ 久（jiǔ）adj. for a long time
e.g., 她哭了很久。

皇帝要他这么做的，他不能不同意。

很快，杨玉环去了道观出家，开始为李隆基的母亲祈福。这个时候她有了一个新的名字，叫杨太真。杨太真在道观见到了高力士，她一看到高力士，就觉得她以前见过这个人。高力士告诉她："那次在花园你见到的男人是皇帝，他很喜欢你，但是由于你是李瑁王爷的王妃，所以皇帝让你先来这里出家，以后再把你接回宫去。"杨玉环听了之后，心里想：原来那个男人是皇帝啊！皇帝的命令①是不能违抗②的，于是她只好同意了。

不久③，李隆基找了一

个好机会，把杨太真接到皇宫里，封①为贵妃②，大家都叫她杨贵妃。李隆基很爱杨贵妃，对她非常好。从此以后，杨贵妃和李隆基过上了幸福的生活。

① 封（fēng）v. confer (a title) upon
e.g., 皇帝封她为皇后。

② 贵妃（guìfēi）n. imperial honored consort
e.g., 贵妃的地位仅次于皇后。

三、李杨共创《霓裳羽衣曲》[1]

李隆基有很多爱好，他喜欢书法①，喜欢听音乐，还喜欢谱曲②。他写的最有名的一首③曲子④是《霓裳羽衣曲》。这首曲子很好听，很多人都喜欢，李隆基自己也特别喜欢。

李隆基刚谱好这个曲子，就把杨贵妃叫来一起听。杨贵妃一听就很喜欢，李隆基特别高兴。杨贵妃边听边说："如果听这个曲子的时候可以看到有人跳舞，应该很好看吧？"李隆基想，杨贵妃这么漂亮，跳舞应该很好看，就说："那你就准备一下这个舞吧。"

杨贵妃很小的时候就学习跳舞。她很聪明，每

① 书法（shūfǎ）n. calligraphy
e.g., 书法是一门艺术。

② 谱曲（pǔqǔ）v. compose music
e.g., 中国的国歌由聂耳谱曲。

③ 首（shǒu）m.w. piece (often used for songs)
e.g., 你为我们唱一首歌吧。

④ 曲子（qǔzi）n. music
e.g., 这首曲子很好听。

天练习这个舞,很快就练好了。她和李隆基再一次听曲子的时候,她就说:"我已经练习好这个舞了,您想看我跳舞吗?"李隆基说:"你这么快就练习好了?那快跳给我看看吧!"

于是,杨贵妃穿上了好看的跳舞的衣服,在李隆基的面前跟着音乐跳起来。杨贵妃跳得非常好,李隆基

① 仙女（xiānnǚ）n. fairy
e.g., 她像天上的仙女一样美丽。

② 着迷（zháomí）adj. fascinated, enchanted
e.g., 幸福没有那么容易，才会特别让人着迷。

③ 珍贵（zhēnguì）adj. precious
e.g., 最珍贵的是人心。

④ 金钗（jīnchāi）n. gold hairpin
e.g., 地上有一根金钗。

⑤ 戴（dài）v. wear
e.g., 你的眼镜别忘了戴。

觉得好像是仙女①在他面前跳舞，看得着了迷②。

李隆基特别高兴，他把一根很珍贵③的金钗④给了杨贵妃，而且亲自把这根金钗戴⑤在杨贵妃的头上。他对后宫的所有人说："这根金钗非常珍贵，应该送给最美的女人。杨贵妃就是最美的女人，所以我要把金钗送给她。"

四、贵妃荔枝飞马送

荔枝①是中国南方产的水果，在北方很少能吃到。李隆基知道杨贵妃最喜欢吃的水果是荔枝之后，他决定给他最喜欢的女人送上她最喜欢的东西，让她高兴。于是他就让人从南方送荔枝来。

荔枝好看又好吃，但很容易烂，不能放太长的时间。长安离南方很远，如果用马车送的话，等荔枝送到就烂了。李隆基希望荔枝送来得越快越好，他问高力士："怎么才能最快地吃到新鲜②的荔枝呢？"

高力士是最懂皇帝的人，他知道皇帝想用最快的

① 荔枝（lìzhī）n. lychee
e.g., 荔枝是很甜、很好吃的水果。

② 新鲜（xīnxian）adj. fresh
e.g., 这个苹果不新鲜了。

办法让<u>杨贵妃</u>吃到荔枝，就说："最快的办法就是在路上建很多驿站[2]，送荔枝的人骑马从南方出发，每到一个站，就换一匹马和一个人送，这样一路不停，很快就能到我们这里了。"皇帝认为这个办法很好，应该很快就能送来好吃的荔枝，就说："那你快去办吧。"

很快，南方的荔枝就送到了长安。杨贵妃看到快马从远处跑来就非常高兴地笑了，因为她知道，她最喜欢吃的荔枝来了。李隆基看到杨贵妃高兴的样子，心里也特别高兴，因为他最喜欢的妃子高兴，他自己就觉得很幸福。

老百姓听说了这件事，都觉得李隆基为了杨贵妃这么做太过分了。当时有一个诗人①写了一首诗，里面就有一句话："一骑红尘妃子笑，无人知是荔枝来。³"

① 诗人（shīrén）n. poet
e.g., 杜甫是唐朝的大诗人。

① 吵架（chǎo jià）v. have a quarrel
e.g., 他们夫妻俩又吵架了。
② 意见（yì jiàn）n. opinion, attitude
e.g., 你有什么意见都可以提。

五、贵妃生气回娘家

李隆基和杨贵妃的感情很好，他们经常在一起，但是他们有时候也会吵架①。一次，杨贵妃和李隆基因为一件小事有了不同的意见②，吵了起来。李隆基很生气，他想，我是皇帝，我是这个国家最重要的人，所有人都要听我

的，<u>杨贵妃</u>你也应该听我的。现在你不听我的，这是对我的不尊重①，我要惩罚②你！他想到的惩罚办法，就是罚<u>杨贵妃</u>回她的娘家。

<u>高力士</u>想了一下，对<u>李隆基</u>说："<u>杨贵妃</u>自己的家已经没有了，她的父亲母亲都已经去世了。现在她的家就是宫里啊，那就让她在宫里接受惩罚吧？"

<u>李隆基</u>当时很生气，不想再见到<u>杨贵妃</u>，想让她离开宫殿，就说："她不是还有个哥哥吗？他哥哥姓<u>杨</u>，她也姓<u>杨</u>，他们是一家人，那就让她回她哥哥家吧，那里也是她的家。"<u>杨贵妃</u>当时已经后悔和皇帝吵架了，但

① 尊重（zūnzhòng）
v. respect
e.g., 学生要尊重老师。

② 惩罚（chéngfá）v.
punish
e.g., 他做错了事，必须受到惩罚。

① 孤单（gūdān）adj. lonely
e.g., 孩子一个人在家,感到很孤单。

是现在皇帝很生气,她只能听皇帝的话回哥哥家了。

　　李隆基让杨贵妃回家之后,心里还是很高兴的,因为他惩罚了杨贵妃。但是以前他都和杨贵妃在一起,现在他觉得自己一个人很孤单①。到了吃饭的时候,李隆基一个人吃饭。饭菜都准备好了之后,他看着菜,心里想：这些菜都是贵妃喜欢吃的啊，以前我们一起吃，现在她不在，这些菜我也不想吃了。

高力士在旁边看到皇帝一直不吃东西，他马上就知道是怎么回事了。以前皇帝每天都是和杨贵妃一边说话一边吃饭的，现在只有皇帝一个人，他怎么能吃好呢？这可怎么办呢？

高力士还没想好办法，就听到皇帝很不高兴地问："今天的饭菜怎么都不好吃啊？你们是怎么做的饭啊？"身边的人都不敢说话，结果皇帝惩罚了好几个人。高力士想来想去，想到了一个好办法。

高力士对李隆基说："杨贵妃今天刚回哥哥家，

① 试（shì）v. test, try
e.g., 你不试怎么知道不会成功呢？

② 态度（tàidu）n. attitude
e.g., 服务态度一定要好。

③ 立刻（lìkè）adv. immediately
e.g., 他立刻站了起来。

她哥哥的家并不是她自己的家，可能很多东西都没有吧，我们要不要送去一些贵妃穿的衣服啊？"高力士是在试试①皇帝的态度②，如果皇帝不同意那就是他现在还生气，如果同意了那就是他不生气了。

这个时候，李隆基心里正想着杨贵妃呢，听高力士一说，马上同意了，然后皇帝就开始吃饭了。吃着吃着，李隆基突然说："我觉得杨贵妃哥哥家里的饭可能不好吃，这些菜都是杨贵妃喜欢吃的，把这里的菜分一半给杨贵妃送去吧。"高力士立刻③把饭菜分了一半给杨贵妃送去。

李隆基现在已经不生

气了，而且还有点想杨贵妃了。高力士看出了皇帝的想法，他知道这个时候皇帝很想把杨贵妃从家里接回来，但是这话不能由皇帝自己说，应该由他说才好。

高力士给杨贵妃哥哥家送去了衣服和饭菜，回来之后对皇帝说："杨贵妃在家里很难过，她知道自己错了，现在正在惩罚自己不吃饭呢！您现在也不吃饭，两个人都不吃饭的话，对身体很不好。我看杨贵妃已经知道自己错了，要不我去把贵妃接回来吧？如果您还觉得生气的话，你可以再惩罚她。"

皇帝听了这话，心里又担心又高兴，担心是因为杨贵妃没有吃饭，高兴是因为杨贵妃知道自己错了。他就说："这样的话，现在就把她接回来吧。"

这个时候已经是晚上了，宫殿的大门已经关上，按照规定是不能再打开的，只能明天再把杨贵妃接回来。但是皇帝很想杨贵妃，如果今天不接回来的话，那今天晚上皇帝就会睡不着觉，所以一定得把杨贵妃接回来。于是，皇帝让高力士把宫殿大门打开，去接杨贵妃。

杨贵妃回来见到李隆基之后，立刻跪①下说："这次都是我的错，我向您道歉，以后我再也不这样了。"

其实②李隆基让高力士去接杨贵妃，就是向杨贵妃认错③了，现在杨贵妃也主动④认错，他觉得杨贵妃真的是太懂事了。两个人分开之后都很想对方，现在都很主动地承认⑤错误，所以之前的问题全都解决了。李隆基很高兴，他把杨贵妃拉起来，说："上次的事情我们都有错，以后我们不要再这样了。"然后他们就高兴地在一起吃饭了。

① 跪（guì）v. kneel
e.g., 她一下子跪在了地上。

② 其实（qíshí）adv. actually
e.g., 你其实不用告诉我这件事。

③ 认错（rèncuò）v. admit mistake
e.g., 我认错，你们惩罚我吧。

④ 主动（zhǔdòng）adv. on one's own initiative
e.g., 她主动要跟我交朋友。

⑤ 承认（chéngrèn）v. admit
e.g., 他承认说过这句话。

① 受宠（shòuchǒng）
v. be in sb's favor
e.g., 电子产品更受宠。

② 消息（xiāoxi）n.
news, information
e.g., 你从哪儿得到的消息？

③ 作为（zuòwéi）v.
act as
e.g., 作为一个老师，我必须严格要求学生。

④ 祝贺（zhùhè）v.
congratulate
e.g., 祝贺你考试得了第一名！

⑤ 赏赐（shǎngcì）v.
reward
e.g., 皇帝赏赐给大臣一件宝贝。

六、杨家受宠①天下乱

皇帝和贵妃吵架又和好的消息②很快就被大家知道了，杨贵妃的三个姐姐作为③家人，都过来祝贺④。李隆基见到杨贵妃的家人非常高兴，给杨贵妃的三个姐姐很多很多的钱。不仅是杨贵妃的姐姐，杨贵妃身边的人也都得到了赏赐⑤。

因为皇帝很喜欢杨贵

妃，所以他每天和杨贵妃在一起。作为一个国家的皇帝，他有很多事情要做，但是他现在都不做了，而是让杨贵妃的哥哥来管理国家。杨贵妃的哥哥叫杨国忠，他很爱钱，而且没有管理国家的能力①。有很多人想当官，他们就给杨国忠送钱。杨国忠收了这

① 能力（nénglì）n. capability
e.g., 他的能力很强。

① 苦（kǔ）adj.
painful, hard
e.g., 他生活得很苦。

② 军队（jūnduì）n.
army
e.g., 这支军队打了很多胜仗。

③ 反叛（fǎnpàn）v.
rebel against
e.g., 你不应该反叛父亲。

④ 叛乱（pànluàn）n.
rebellion, revolt
e.g., 这场叛乱持续了很长时间。

⑤ 借口（jièkǒu）n.
excuse
e.g., 不要为自己的失败找借口。

⑥ 抓（zhuā）v.
capture
e.g., 大家一起抓住了小偷。

些人的钱，让很多没有能力的人当了官，所以老百姓的生活越来越苦①。

无论杨贵妃想要什么，李隆基都会给她。当时，为杨贵妃做衣服的就有七百人。还有她吃的荔枝，每年都专门派人从南方送来。在这样的情况下，国家出现了很多问题。

安禄山和史思明是唐朝的两个大官，他们带着十五万军队②反叛③，这场叛乱④叫"安史之乱4"。他们的借口⑤是要抓⑥住杨国忠，由他们来管理国家，这样国家的问题就解决了。

皇帝听说军队发生了叛乱，很生气也很害怕，带着杨贵妃和她的哥哥姐姐离开了长安，逃①向四川。这是一条很长的路，到马嵬坡这个地方的时候，突然发生了一件大事。

皇帝的士兵们认为，国家出现问题都是因为杨贵妃和她的哥哥。现在皇帝带着他们去四川，国家还会由杨国忠来管理，问题还是得不到解决。所以士兵们一起动手，把杨国

① 逃（táo）v.
escape
e.g., 小偷逃走了。

忠杀了。

听到这个消息，李隆基和杨贵妃都很吃惊，因为这个事情太突然了。之前他们一直希望快点到四川，然后他们就能一起开始新的生活。李隆基知道杨国忠做了很多不好的事情，但是他没想到士兵们会动手把杨国忠杀了。

　　杨贵妃很难过，她哭了起来。这么多年来，她和她的哥哥关系很好，现在她的哥哥突然被杀死了，她又失去①了一位亲人②。这个时候她看着李隆基，李隆基也看着她，他们都很担心这些士兵下一步要做什么。

① 失去（shīqù）v.
lose
e.g., 我不想失去你。

② 亲人（qīnrén）n.
one's family members
e.g., 他在这个城市没有亲人。

① 根本（gēnběn）n. root, essence
e.g., 你要从根本上考虑这个问题。

七、贵妃魂断马嵬坡

士兵们杀了杨国忠之后，事情并没有完。他们认为，杨国忠并不是国家问题的根本①，国家问题的根本是杨贵妃。杨贵妃在皇帝身边，皇帝就没有时间管理国家。如果没有了杨贵妃，皇帝就能好好地管理国家了。于是士兵们要求皇帝杀了杨贵妃，然后才能前进。

皇帝看着这些士兵，他们一直在他身边，听他的话，他们都是很好的士兵。现在这些士兵想杀了杨贵妃，他不敢相信这是真的。但是他也知道，现在必须要做出决定。

李隆基看了看杨贵妃，

又看了看士兵们，心里想：杨贵妃是我最喜欢的妃子，我们在一起生活了十几年了，我不能杀死她啊！他又看着高力士，说："你能不能让他们不要这样做啊？"

高力士无奈①地看着皇帝，流着泪②说："这些士兵已经决定了，如果不杀了杨贵妃的话，他们是不会前进的。这个时候我们只能听他们的。"

听了高力士的话，杨贵妃流下了眼泪。她知道高力士说的话是真的，现在皇帝也得听士兵的话。杨贵妃对李隆基说："皇上，为了国家，我还是去死吧，您多保重③！"

李隆基和杨贵妃一起

① 无奈（wúnài）
v. have no choice, cannot help but
e.g., 看到你这么伤心，我也很无奈。

② 流泪（liúlèi）v. weep
e.g., 她看着孩子默默流泪。

③ 保重（bǎozhòng）
v. take care
e.g., 你一定要保重身体，不要太累了。

① 自杀（zìshā）v. kill oneself
e.g., 他的女朋友跳楼自杀了。

② 梨树（líshù）n. pear tree
e.g., 院子里有一棵梨树。

③ 布（bù）n. cloth
e.g., 我买一块布做衣服。

大哭起来，他们哭了很久。李隆基对士兵说："我不想让你们杀了杨贵妃，还是让她自杀①吧。"

于是，高力士把杨贵妃带走了，杨贵妃在一棵梨树②上上吊自杀了，这个时候杨贵妃三十八岁。李隆基看到高力士拿回的杨贵妃上吊用的白布③，哭得非常伤心。

杨国忠和杨贵妃都死了以后，士兵们出发了，很快就到了四川。

① 结束（jiéshù）v.
end
e.g., 电影结束了，我们走出了电影院。

八、李隆基独思杨贵妃

一直到安史之乱结束①，李隆基都住在四川。他很难过，每天都不怎么说话，也不怎么吃饭，什么事也没办法让他高兴起来，因为没有了杨贵妃。高力士知道李隆基一直在难过，他很想让皇帝忘了杨贵妃，但是这是不可能的。杨贵妃是李隆基最喜欢的妃子，他们在一起幸福生活了十几年，皇帝忘不了她。

过了一年多，安史之乱结束了，李隆基回到了长安的宫殿里。这个时候他已经不是皇帝了，他现在是太上皇[5]，他的儿子是皇帝。再次回到他生活了十几年的宫殿里，李隆基在做所有事情的时候都会想到杨贵妃。吃饭的时候，他想到了杨贵妃和他一起吃饭时高兴的样子；出去看花的时候，他想到了杨贵妃比花还好看的脸；下雨的时候，他想到了他和杨贵妃一起看雨的日子。现在宫殿里的一切都跟以前一样，但是少了杨贵妃，

<u>李隆基</u>觉得这里所有的东西都跟以前不一样了。

<u>李隆基</u>不再是皇帝,也不用做管理国家的事情,所以他更想<u>杨贵妃</u>了。虽然这个时候他的身边还有很多妃子,但是他心里只想着<u>杨贵妃</u>。于是他让人画了一张<u>杨贵妃</u>的画像。

之后，李隆基每天早上起来第一件事就是看这张画像。看着杨贵妃的画像，他就感觉杨贵妃还在他身边。吃饭的时候，他看着画像，这样他就感觉杨贵妃和他一起吃饭。出去散步的时候，他也带着杨贵妃的画像，这样就感觉杨贵妃和他一起散步①。

高力士看到李隆基现在每天拿着杨贵妃的画像，对什么事都不感兴趣②，心里很着急③。他想了很多办法，都不能让李隆基高兴起来。虽然这样，高力士还是一直在想办法。

① 散步（sànbù）v.
take a walk
e.g., 吃完饭我们出门散步。

② 兴趣（xìngqù）v.
be interested in
e.g., 你对画画有兴趣吗？

③ 着急（zháojí）v.
worry
e.g., 不要着急，慢慢来。

九、道士仙界寻贵妃

有一天，高力士听说有一个道士⁶可以找到人的魂魄⁷。他想，如果这个道士能找到杨贵妃的魂魄，让皇帝和杨贵妃的魂魄见面，让他们说说话，这样皇帝就能好起来了吧？于是他找到了这个道士，把这个道士带到了李隆基那里。

李隆基正在一个人看着画中的杨贵妃。他看到高力士带着一个道士进来，就说："高力士，你知道我现在不喜欢有人在这里，怎么还带着人进来？"高力士说："我听说这位道士能找到死去的人的魂魄，我想让他把杨贵妃的魂魄找到和您见面，您觉得怎么样？"高力士说完，又看着道士说："他已经找到了很多人的魂魄了。"

　　李隆基第一次听说这样的事情，有点不相信，但是他很想杨贵妃，所以他决定试一试。

　　晚上吃完饭之后，李隆基和高力士都做好了准备，看着那个道士开始找

魂魄。道士先去了地府[8]，因为人死了魂魄就要去地府。他在那里找了很久也没有找到。

　　道士回来之后告诉李隆基说："杨贵妃死后没有去地府，我在地府里没找到她的魂魄。我现在再去天上看看吧。"听了道士的话，李隆基心想：人死了不都是去地府的吗？他说地府里没有，那就是说杨贵妃没死？他看了看高力士，高力士说："他说去天上看看，我们就等着吧。"

过了好久，那道士又回来了，说："我刚才去天上了，问了天上的人，他们说杨贵妃也不在天上。不过有一个人告诉我，他在蓬莱岛见过杨贵妃，让我去那里找她，我现在就去看看。"

道士很快到了蓬莱岛，岛上有很多神仙①。很快，他就发现了杨贵妃，她现在是一名仙女。因为杨贵妃跳舞跳得很好，所以死后她没有去地府，而是被神仙带到了蓬莱岛上，成

① 神仙（shénxiān）n. immortal
e.g., 神仙可以长生不老。

了跳舞的仙女。

道士告诉杨贵妃："人间的李隆基在你死后一直很想你,每天饭也吃不下,觉也睡不好,生活得很不好,所以我想带你去看看他,可以吗?"

杨贵妃很想去看李隆基。但是现在她是仙女,不能去人间,于是她拿出了当年李隆基给她的金钗,

对道士说:"我也很想见皇帝,但是我现在不能去见他。这是当年他给我的金钗,我一直带在身边,你见到他之后把金钗给他,他就知道我很想他了。"

道士回来后把金钗给了李隆基。李隆基看到这根金钗的时候,才真正地相信这个道士说的话。他知道杨贵妃现在在蓬莱岛当了仙女,心里很高兴,但也更想她了。

十、李隆基月宫见贵妃

玉帝听说李隆基让道士到处找杨贵妃的魂魄的故事，觉得他们很可怜，就想让他们一直在一起。

每年的八月十五，月宫要举行一次宴会①。杨贵妃要在这一年的宴会上跳舞，于是玉帝让道士带李隆基来参加这次宴会。

李隆基正在宫里看着金钗的时候，道士来了，说："玉帝让我八月十五带您去参加月宫的宴会，宴会上杨贵妃会跳舞，到时候你们就可以见面了。"李隆基非常高兴，每天等着八月十五的到来。

终于到了八月十五这一天，道士带着李隆基去

① 宴会（yànhuì）n. banquet
e.g., 宴会在我们市最好的饭店举行。

了月宫，杨贵妃也从蓬莱岛来到了月宫。

月宫的宴会很快就开始了，杨贵妃跳起舞来。她跳舞时用的音乐就是当年的《霓裳羽衣曲》，她的舞跳得比当年还要好。跳完后，杨贵妃被带到了李隆基面前。

杨贵妃不知道李隆基来月宫找她，当她看到李隆基的时候，突然说不出话了，因为她每天都想的李隆基就在她面前，她有点不相信这是真的。

李隆基也没有说话，他抓住了杨贵妃的手，心里又高兴又难过，高兴的是见到了自己天天想的人，难过的是想起了当年杨贵妃的

死。他想说点什么，但是想了很久也没想好，所以他什么也没说，就是看着<u>杨贵妃</u>，心里十分高兴。

<u>杨贵妃</u>也特别高兴，她看着<u>李隆基</u>，眼泪止不住地流了下来。

"是你吗？"

"就是我！"

"你是怎么来的？"

"<u>玉帝</u>知道我一直在想你，就让我来看看你，没想到真的见到你了。当年没能救你，我心里很难过，也很后悔，这些年我一直很想见你。"

"我也很想你啊，我自杀后有人带我去了<u>蓬莱岛</u>，我一直生活在那里。我一直想你，但是见不到你，所以我每天都看着你给我的金钗。"

"你死了之后我让人画了你的画像，我每天都看着画上的你，就好像你在我身边一样，没想到我现在真的见到你了。"

李隆基和杨贵妃说了很多话，感觉怎么说都说不完。李隆基很想让杨贵妃和自己回到人间，不想自己一个人回去。杨贵妃也想跟着李隆基去人间，这样他们就能在一起了。

正在他们难过的时候，玉帝告诉他们，来到了月宫就不要再回去了，就住在月宫吧。

李隆基和杨贵妃高兴

地在<u>月宫</u>住下了,一直生活在一起,不再分开。

[1] 霓裳羽衣曲（Nícháng Yǔyī Qǔ）Raiment of Rainbows and Feathers
中国唐代宫廷乐舞。传说是唐玄宗李隆基所作，由他宠爱的贵妃杨玉环作舞表演。
The imperial dance accompanied by music from China's Tang Dynasty. It's said to have been composed by a Tang emperor, Li Longji, and performed by his most beloved consort, Yang Yuhuan.

[2] 驿站（yìzhàn）Courier Station
古时专供传递文书者或来往官吏中途住宿、补给、换马的处所。
The place where messengers or officials stop for accommodation, replenishment or to switch horses.

[3] 一骑红尘妃子笑，无人知是荔枝来（Yí jì hóngchén fēizi xiào, wú rén zhī shì lìzhī lái）
快马扬起尘土飞奔而来，贵妃笑脸相迎，没有人知道送来的是荔枝。本诗讽刺了杨贵妃穷奢极欲的生活。
A quote from a famous Tang poem used to satirize the extravagant life of Yang Guifei.

[4] 安史之乱（Ān-shǐ zhī luàn）An-Shi Rebellion
是中国唐代发生的一场政治叛乱，由安禄山与史思明发动，所以叫"安史之乱"。这也是唐朝由盛而衰的转折点。
A political rebellion during the Tang Dynasty. Since it was launched by generals An Lushan and Shi Siming, this revolt is called the An-Shi Rebellion. It marked the beginning of Tang's decline.

[5] 太上皇（tàishàng huáng）Emperor Emeritus
太上皇，又称太上皇帝，是中国历史上给予退位皇帝或当朝皇帝在世父亲的头衔，通常给予的对象是在世但已禅位的皇帝。
Common designation of an abdicated emperor during his remaining years, particularly during the reign of a son.

[6] 道士（dàoshi）Toaist Priest
道士是中国道教的神职人员。
The clergymen of Chinese Taoism.

[7] 魂魄（húnpò）Soul
在中国古人想象中附在人体内可以脱离人体存在的精神，在人体内人就活着，脱离了人体人就死亡。
The spirit which can exist even if it is separated from the human body. If the spirit is in the human body, people are alive; when it leaves the body, people die.

English Version

Four Ancient Beauties: Yang Guifei

1. First Encounter

More than a thousand years ago, during the Tang Dynasty, there was an emperor whose personal name was Li Longji. He reigned for a few decades and was very accomplished in governing his country.

When he was in his fifties, his favorite concubine died of illness, which greatly saddened Li Longji. He was always feeling low in mood. Gao Lishi, one of his eunuchs, tried his best to please the emperor.

One fine day, flowers were all in blossom in the imperial garden. Knowing that the emperor enjoyed flowers, Gao Lishi proposed, "Your Majesty, would you like to go to the garden and see the flowers?" Li Longji replied, "Sounds good. Flowers are now blooming. Let's go see them."

It happened that a woman was resting in the garden. When she saw two men walking toward where she was, she got shy and hid half of her face behind a flower and walked away.

When Li Longji saw her, he noticed that she was extremely pretty, prettier than the flower she used to hide her face. Gao Lishi also felt that she was the prettiest woman he had ever seen.

The woman turned her head and looked back. Her eyes met with Li Longji's. She smiled and then walked away slowly. Li Longji was delighted, and from her smile he deemed this woman liked him. Li Longji stood where he was, looking at the woman until she was out of sight.

2. Li Longji Finding a Way to Marry Yang Yuhuan

Gao Lishi knew what was on Li Longji's mind. He would always quickly know what the emperor was thinking about and what he wanted to do. Gao would then meet the emperor's needs without having to be told what to do. This was the reason why Li Longji always kept Gao by his side.

Gao Lishi soon discovered that the woman they had seen in the garden was Yang Yuhuan, the wife of Li Mao, son of Li Longji. How could this happen? Among all the pretty women in the world, the emperor liked only this one woman who was none other than his son's wife! This would make things difficult. If other people knew about this, they would think the emperor was acting dubiously. Being the emperor's best confidant, Gao Lishi knew that it was not easy for the emperor to find someone he liked. Gao had to endeavor to find a solution for the emperor. It had to be a solution that allowed the emperor to keep Yang Yuhuan as his own in a justifiable way.

Gao Lishi thought hard for a few days and finally came up with a solution. He went to see the emperor immediately. "Your Majesty, do you remember the woman we met in the garden?" Li Longji was very pleased with the mention of the woman. "Indeed, Gao Lishi is really my best confidant and knows what I want. He must have found that woman," Li Longji thought to himself. He asked, "Have you found the woman? She is pretty, yes, I like her." Gao replied, "Your Majesty, I did find her. Her name is Yang Yuhuan and she is Prince Li Mao's wife."

Li Longji was displeased after hearing this. He thought, "Li Mao's wife? Well, if this is the case, she will not be mine."

Seeing Li Longji was quite unhappy, Gao Lishi said at once, "Yang Yuhuan is Prince Li Mao's wife for now, but in the near future she won't be. She will be yours." Li Longji was eager to hear the solution and asked, "How is this possible? Speak up."

Gao said, "You could make an arrangement to pray for your mother, which requires a woman to become a Taoist nun to do the praying. You could then ask Prince Li Mao to allow his wife to leave the imperial palace and go to the Taoist temple. In this way, Yang Yuhuan will no longer be Prince Li Mao's wife."

Li Longji did not think this was a solution at all. He said, "You call that a solution? If she goes to a Taoist temple, I won't be able to see her then either. It will not work."

Realizing the emperor didn't agree to this solution, Gao Lishi explained, "After Yang Yuhuan goes to the temple and becomes a Taoist nun, she will have a new name. No one will know her and no one will ever know she used to be the wife of a prince. After some time, when people forget about this praying thing, you can get her back from the temple. I think it will work."

Li Longji nodded his agreement and said, "This works. You are really smart! But I think Li Mao won't be happy, and he might not agree to this. I shall find him a new wife."

Gao Lishi said, "Great! I will approach Prince Li Mao first. I will let him know about the praying and ask him to see you."

Li Mao was not happy and not willing to see his wife become a nun in a Taoist temple, even if he could have a new wife. But it was the emperor's decision and he could not disagree with the emperor.

Soon Yang Yuhuan went to the Taoist temple and became a nun, praying for Li Longji's mother. She received a new name, Yang Taizhen. In the Taoist temple, she met with Gao Lishi and recognized him as someone she had seen before. Gao Lishi told her, "In the garden our emperor saw you, and he likes you. But since you are Prince Li Mao's wife, the emperor decided that you should first stay here as a nun. After some time he will have you return to the palace." Yang Yuhuan thought to herself, "It was the emperor that I met!" She knew she could not disobey the emperor's order. She had no choice but to agree.

Not long after this, Li Longji took an opportunity to bring Yang Taizhen back to the imperial palace and gave her the title Guifei, or Imperial Honored Consort. Li Longji loved her deeply and treated her quite well. From then onwards, she was known as Yang Guifei, and they started a happy life together.

3. *Raiment of Rainbows and Feathers,* Music by Li and Dance by Yang

Li Longji made many accomplishments, including calligraphy and music. He could compose music. One of his most well-known pieces was *Raiment of Rainbows and Feathers.* It was a very beautiful piece, and many people liked it, including of course Li Longji himself.

As soon as Li Longji had finished this piece, he asked Guifei to listen to it with him. Guifei immediately liked it, which greatly pleased Li Longji. While listening, Guifei said, "If there was someone dancing to the music, it would be extremely beautiful, wouldn't it?" Li Longji thought that his charming Guifei should be able to dance beautifully. So he said, "Why don't you dance, accompanied by my music?"

Yang Guifei had learned how to dance when she was quite young. She started to choreograph a dance to Li Longji's piece and practice it every day. Being a very smart lady, she quickly finished her work. One day when she was listening to the music with Li Longji again, she said, "I am ready to dance for you. Would you like to see it?" Li Longji was amazed, "You are ready so very soon! Please do dance for me."

Yang Guifei put on a beautiful costume and danced in front of Li Longji with his music for accompaniment. She danced so well that Li Longji was enchanted, feeling it was a fairy that was dancing for him.

Li Longji was so pleased he rewarded Guifei with a rare and precious gold hairpin, and embellished Guifei's hair with it himself. He then told all the ladies in his inner palace, "This gold hairpin is very rare and should be granted to the prettiest and loveliest woman. Guifei is the prettiest and loveliest woman, and I give it to her."

4. Express Delivery of Lychees for Guifei

The lychee is a tropical fruit native to southern China, and rarely found in the north. When Li Longji learned that Guifei's favorite fruit was lychees, he decided to please his woman by supplying her with what she liked most and have lychees delivered from the south.

Fresh lychees are pleasing to the eye, and very sweet and flavorful, but they are difficult to store and can easily go bad.

Chang'an was a northern city and lychees would certainly go rotten if they were delivered by carriage. Wishing that lychees could be delivered as fast as possible, Li Longji asked Gao Lishi, "How can we get fresh lychees in the fastest way?"

Gao Lishi, who knew the emperor well, understood that the emperor wanted to use the fastest methods so that his consort could enjoy her favorite fruit. Gao said, "The best way is to build a number of courier stations. Lychees can be delivered by the imperial courier's fast horses. The riders and horses can take shifts day and night, and the fruit can be delivered non-stop to the capital." The emperor agreed that this was the best way to deliver fresh lychees and said, "Do as you've suggested then."

Soon enough, lychees from the south were delivered to Chang'an. Yang Guifei could not help smiling when she saw from a distance horses galloping towards the palace, for she knew that she would soon be able to enjoy the fresh fruit. Seeing his consort happy, Li Longji was pleased and happiness filled his heart.

The ordinary people believed that Li Longji had gone too far to please his consort. In one Tang poem, there is a line depicting this: "Raising dust on the way, a fast horse gallops by; no one knows lychees are being delivered, which pleases the concubine."

5. Guifei Moving to Her Brother's Home After a Quarrel

Li Longji and Yang Guifei loved each other so much that they spent most of their time together. But they did sometimes have disagreements. One day, they disagreed with each other over something trivial and had a quarrel. Li Longji was annoyed. He thought to himself, "I am the emperor and the most important person in this country. Everybody should obey me, and Guifei is no exception. Now Guifei, you dared to quarrel with me, and you are not respectful. I will have to punish you!" He figured out a way to punish Guifei, which was to dispel her from the palace to where she had lived before she was married.

Gao Lishi gave it a thought and said to the emperor, "Yang Guifei has no home of her own. Her parents are both deceased. Her home is here in the palace. You could let her stay in the palace and punish her all the same."

But at that time Li Longji was so angry he did not want to see Guifei again and wanted to banish her from the palace. He said, "Doesn't she have a brother? They have the same family name; they are family. Let her go to her brother's home. That is her home too." Guifei regretted quarreling with the emperor, but the emperor was angry. She had no choice but to go to her brother's home.

In the beginning, Li Longji felt glad he had punished his consort by letting her return home. But soon Li Longji began to feel lonely, as he was so used to being with Guifei. At dinner, he sat at the table alone. Looking at all the delicacies, he thought to himself, "These are all Guifei's favorite dishes. We shared these dishes before. Now that she is not here, I don't want to have them all by myself."

Gao Lishi was waiting on the emperor and realized what was on the emperor's mind. Before, when the emperor would have dinner with Yang Guifei, he would enjoy both the dishes and Guifei's company. Now that he was alone, he had lost his appetite. What could be done?

Before Gao Lishi could think of anything, the emperor started to speak in an unhappy voice, "Why do the dishes taste so bad today? What a miserable job you've done!" People around him were too scared to speak. Even so, the emperor punished a few people out of rage. After thinking for a while, Gao came up with a good idea.

Gao Lishi said to Li Longji, "Yang Guifei arrived at her brother's today. It is not her own home there, probably she's in want of a few things. Could we take some of her clothes to her?" By saying this, Gao Lishi intended to test the emperor's attitude. If the emperor did not allow him to take anything to Guifei, he might still be angry. If the emperor agreed, he might not be angry any more.

Li Longji was actually thinking of Yang Guifei at that moment. He immediately agreed to what Gao Lishi said. Then he started to eat. Before long, all of a sudden he said, "Dishes at Guifei's brother's home may not taste very good. All these here are what Guifei likes. Take half of them to Guifei." Gao Lishi did as the emperor told him immediately.

Li Longji was not angry anymore. Instead he started to miss Yang Guifei. Gao Lishi understood this and was sure the emperor wanted to have Guifei back at the palace, but apparently the emperor could not simply say this. Gao Lishi would have to say it for him.

Gao Lishi brought clothes and food to Yang Guifei and returned to the palace. He told the emperor, "Yang Guifei is very sad. She knows she did wrong and is punishing herself by not taking any food. And your Majesty is not eating either. This is harmful to your health. Since Yang Guifei is regretful, why not let me bring her back to the palace? You could punish her when she comes back, if you are still angry."

The emperor was worried that Yang Guifei was refusing to eat. But he was also pleased that Guifei was regretful. He said, "Well, you can go and get her back now."

It was already late in the day; the palace gate was closed. It was a rule that once the gate was closed, it could not be re-opened for the day. In this case, Yang Guifei would have to return to the palace the next day. But the emperor missed his consort so much; he would find it hard to go to sleep if Guifei did not come back that day. He decided that Guifei had to be brought back without delay, so he ordered Gao Lishi to open the gate and bring Yang Guifei back.

Yang Guifei kneeled to the emperor when she returned, saying, "It was all my fault. I apologize. I will never quarrel with you again."

By having Gao Lishi bring Guifei back, Li Longji actually admitted his mistake. Now that Yang Guifei had apologized, he felt that Guifei was really considerate and empathetic. This short separation made them miss each other, and they both admitted their own mistakes, so the bad feelings were completely dismissed. Glad as Li Longji was, he helped Guifei up and said, "We were both wrong. Let's not be like that again." They then happily went for their dinner together.

6. Excessive Favoritism to the Yangs Leading to Turmoil in the Country

Soon everybody came to know that the emperor and his consort had made up after their quarrel. The three sisters of Guifei came to the palace to congratulate the emperor and Guifei. Li Longji was pleased to see Guifei's family, and gifted them a lot of money. Li Longji also rewarded all those who were waiting on Guifei.

The emperor favored Guifei so much that he spent most of his time with her. He should have had a great many things to do governing his country, but he had no time for that. Instead, he empowered Guifei's brother, Yang Guozhong, to run the country for him. Yang Guozhong was greedy and not capable of running a country. There were people who bribed Yang Guozhong in exchange for official positions. Yang let many incapable people become officials. As a result, ordinary people's lives worsened.

Whatever Yang Guifei desired, Li Longji would give her. As many as 700 tailors and seamstresses made clothes for Yang Guifei. Lychees, her favorite fruit, were delivered from the south by the imperial couriers each year. Gradually many social problems appeared in the country.

An Lushan and Shi Siming were high-ranking officials in the Tang Dynasty. Leading 150 thousand soldiers, they rebelled. This was known as the An-Shi Rebellion. The excuse for the rebellion was to arrest Yang Guozhong. An and Shi would then take over the responsibilities of running the country. This, according to them, would solve the problems the country was having.

The rebellion both angered and scared the emperor. He decided to flee from Chang'an and go to Sichuan Province with Yang Guifei and her brother and sisters. It was a long way from Chang'an to Sichuan. When they arrived at a place called Mawei Po, an unexpected change occurred.

The emperor's soldiers believed that all the problems were due to Yang Guifei and her brother. The emperor wanted to go to Sichuan, but the country would still be run by Yang Guozhong, the problems would not be solved. So the soldiers launched an attack and killed Yang Guozhong.

Hearing the news, Li Longji and Yang Guifei were shocked. It happened so suddenly. They had hoped that they could arrive in Sichuan quickly and start a new life together. Li Longji knew that Yang Guozhong had done many bad things, but he never thought Yang would be killed by the soldiers.

Yang Guifei wept. She had been very close to her brother over all these years. Now he was killed and she had lost her closest family member. She looked at Li Longji, and Li Longji looked at her. They were both worried as to what the soldiers would do next.

7. The Death of Yang Guifei at Mawei Po

The soldiers indeed did not stop there after they killed Yang Guozhong. Yang Guozhong was not the root cause of all the problems, they believed. Yang Guifei was. With Yang Guifei by the emperor's side, the emperor had neither the time nor the will to govern his country. They had to get rid of Yang Guifei. Then the emperor would focus on governing his country. The soldiers asked the emperor to kill Yang Guifei, otherwise they would refuse to continue the journey to Sichuan.

The emperor looked at his soldiers. They had followed him for years and had been very loyal. They were good soldiers, but now they wanted to kill his Guifei. He just could not believe what he heard. Yet he knew he had to make a decision.

Li Longji looked at Yang Guifei, and then looked at the soldiers, thinking, "Guifei is my favorite consort and we've lived together for more than ten years. How could I kill her?" He turned his head to Gao Lishi and asked, "Can't you stop these soldiers?"

Gao Lishi looked at the emperor, helpless and crying. He said, "Your Majesty, these soldiers have made up their mind. If you do not let Yang Guifei die, they will not continue on. We have no choice but to listen to them."

Hearing what Gao Lishi said, Yang Guifei started to weep. She understood that what Gao Lishi said was true, and the emperor would have to listen to the soldiers. Yang Guifei said to Li Longji, "Your Majesty, let me die, for the sake of your country. Please take good care of yourself."

Both of them cried for a long time. Finally Li Longji told the soldiers, "I won't allow you to kill her. Let Guifei do it herself."

Gao Lishi took Yang Guifei away to a pear tree. Yang Guifei hanged herself on the tree. She died at the age of 38. Gao Lishi brought back to Li Longji the white silk cloth Guifei used to hang herself. Li Longji wept inconsolably.

Now that both Yang Guozhong and Yang Guifei were dead, the soldiers embarked on their trip. Soon the emperor and his soldiers arrived in Sichuan.

8. Li Longji Missing Yang Guifei

Li Longji lived in Sichuan until the An-Shi Rebellion was over. He was sad and did not say much, nor did he eat much. Nothing could make him interested or happy, as Yang Guifei was not with him anymore. Gao Lishi knew Li Longji was sad and tried hard to console the emperor. But it was impossible for the emperor to forget Yang Guifei, his favorite consort, with whom he had lived for more than a decade.

After the end of the An-Shi Rebellion more than a year later, Li Longji returned to his palace in Chang'an. He gave up the throne to his son and was no longer the emperor. Living in the palace where he lived with Yang Guifei before, everything he did reminded him of Yang Guifei. When he would have dinner, he would recall the happy moments of them having dinner together. When he would go to the garden to look at the flowers, he would think of Yang Guifei, prettier than any flower. When it would rain, he would think of the rainy days he spent with Guifei. Everything in the palace remained the same, except there was no Yang Guifei around. That really made the difference for Li Longji.

Li Longji was no longer the emperor and was spared from governing his country. All he was thinking about was Yang Guifei. He had a number of concubines, but Yang Guifei was the only one that he was thinking of. He commissioned a portrait of Yang Guifei.

In time the portrait was completed, and first thing each morning, Li Longji would look at the portrait, feeling Guifei was beside him. When he had dinner, he would look at the portrait, assuming Guifei was with him at the table. When he took a walk outside, he would even bring the portrait with him, as if he had Yang Guifei's company.

Gao Lishi was worried that Li Longji had lost interest in everything. He would only gaze at Yang Guifei's portrait. He tried many different things but to no avail. However, Gao Lishi did not give up.

9. Guifei Found by a Taoist Priest

One day Gao Lishi heard that there was a Taoist priest who could find souls of the dead. He thought, "If this priest can find Yang Guifei's soul, His Majesty could meet with her soul, and they could have a chat. In this way His Majesty may recover from his current state." Gao Lishi found the priest and took him to Li

Longji.

Li Longji was again looking at the portrait of Yang Guifei. When he saw the priest, he asked Gao Lishi, "You know I do not like people to be around me, why bring someone here?" Gao Lishi replied, "I heard that this priest can find dead people's souls. I would like him to find Yang Guifei's soul so you can meet her. How does that sound?" Gao Lishi looked at the priest and told Li Longji, "He has found the souls of a great many people."

Li Longji had never heard of such a thing and he did not believe it. However, he missed Yang Guifei desperately and wanted to have a try.

In the evening after dinner, both Li Longji and Gao Lishi were ready to watch how the priest would find the soul of Yang Guifei. The priest went to the Netherworld first, as souls went there when people died. The priest spent a lot of time there, but could not find Yang Guifei's soul.

He returned and told Li Longji, "Yang Guifei did not go to the Netherworld, as I could not find her there. Now I will go to Heaven to have a try." Upon hearing this, Li Longji thought to himself, "Doesn't everybody go to the Netherworld when dead? Since Guifei is not in the Netherworld, does it mean Guifei is not dead?" He looked at Gao Lishi and Gao said, "Let's just wait until the priest goes to Heaven."

After a long while, the priest returned, saying, "I went to Heaven and asked about Yang Guifei. I could not find her there either, but someone told me that they saw her on Penglai Island. So I will now go to Penglai Island."

The priest soon arrived at the island. There were many

immortals living on the island. He did find Yang Guifei. She was a fairy there. As Yang Guifei was an excellent dancer, she did not go to the Netherworld, but was brought to Penglai Island by an immortal, and became a dancing fairy.

The priest told Yang Guifei, "Since you died, Li Longji in the human world has been missing you all the time. He cannot eat, he cannot sleep, and he lives a miserable life. Would you like to see him?"

Yang Guifei really wanted to see Li Longji, but she could not. She was a fairy and could not go to the human world. She took out the gold hairpin Li Longji gave her many years before and said to the priest, "I'd like to see the emperor, but I cannot. This is something he gave me. I have never parted with it. Now please take it back to him. He will know how much I have missed him."

The priest brought the gold hairpin back to Li Longji. Seeing the hairpin, Li Longji finally believed what the priest said. He was glad that Yang Guifei had become a fairy on Penglai Island, but in his heart he missed her even more.

10. Reunion at the Moon Palace

When the Jade Emperor heard that Li Longji had asked the priest to help find Yang Guifei's soul in various places, he took pity on the couple and decided to make arrangements so that they could live together again.

Every year, on the fifteenth day of the eighth lunar month, at the Moon Palace there was a banquet. This year Yang Guifei would perform a dance at the banquet. The Jade Emperor told the priest that he could bring Li Longji to the banquet.

Li Longji was looking at the gold hairpin when the priest came and told him, "The Jade Emperor has asked me to take you to the banquet at the Moon Palace, where Yang Guifei will dance. You will be able to meet then." Li Longji was extremely delighted and eagerly waited for the day to come.

The day finally came. Li Longji was brought to the Moon Palace by the priest, and Yang Guifei also arrived at the Moon Palace from Penglai Island.

The banquet soon began. Yang Guifei began her dance to *Raiment of Rainbows and Feathers.* Her performance was even better than years before. After her performance, she was brought to where Li Longji sat.

Yang Guifei had no idea that Li Longji had come to the Moon Palace. When she saw him, she was speechless. Every day she had wished to see him again, and she could not believe that her dream had come true.

Li Longji was also speechless. He held Yang Guifei's hands and had mixed feelings. He was so glad that he was able to meet this person he missed so dearly. He was also saddened by the memory of her tragic death. He longed to say something. He tried for a while but failed to find any words. He gave up trying to speak, just looked closely at Guifei, overwhelmed with happiness.

Yang Guifei was also greatly delighted. She looked at Li Longji and tears streamed down her cheeks.

"Is that you?"

"Yes, it's me."

"How did you come here?"

"The Jade Emperor knows that I miss you so much, so he allowed me to see you here. I am so happy I am finally seeing you again! I am very sad and regret that I could not save you years ago. I have been missing you ever since."

"I miss you dearly too. After I killed myself, I was taken to Penglai Island and have lived there ever since. I wanted to see you again so much, but I could not. All I could do is look at the gold hairpin you gave me, each and every day."

"After you died, I had your portrait painted for me. I looked at your portrait every day, as if you were with me. I never expected that I would see you again."

Li Longji and Yang Guifei talked on and on. They could not stop. Li Longji wished Yang Guifei could go back to the human world with him, and he did not want to return all by himself. Yang Guifei also wished she could follow Li Longji to the human world so that they could be together.

When they were feeling sad that they could not be together, the Jade Emperor told them that they could actually stay at the Moon Palace and live there.

Li Longji and Yang Guifei thus happily stayed at the Moon Palace. Ever since then, they have been living together and have never parted again.

一、选择题。Choose the correct answer according to the story.

1. 最懂李隆基的人是谁？（　　）

   A. 高力士　　B. 杨贵妃　　C. 杨国忠　　D. 道士

2. 杨贵妃最开始叫什么名字？（　　）

   A. 杨贵妃　　B. 杨太真　　C. 杨国忠　　D. 杨玉环

3. 杨贵妃原来是谁的王妃？（　　）

   A. 高力士　　B. 李瑁　　C. 李隆基　　D. 杨国忠

4. 杨玉环去道观做什么？（　　）

   A. 游玩　　　　　　B. 为李隆基的母亲祈福

   C. 去见李瑁　　　　D. 看花

5. 杨玉环是在哪里出家的？（　　）

   A. 梨园　　B. 宫殿　　C. 道观　　D. 蓬莱岛

6. 李隆基认为杨贵妃是最美的女人，把什么东西给了她？（　　）

   A. 帽子　　B. 衣服　　C. 花　　D. 金钗

7. 杨贵妃喜欢吃什么水果？（　　）

   A. 荔枝　　B. 苹果　　C. 西瓜　　D. 梨

8. 杨贵妃的哥哥叫什么名字?（　　）

　　A. 杨玉环　　B. 李隆基　　C. 杨国忠　　D. 高力士

9. 安史之乱的时候,李隆基和杨贵妃他们逃向了哪里?
（　　）

　　A. 长安　　　B. 四川　　　C. 地府　　　D. 蓬莱岛

10. 杨贵妃死在哪里?（　　）

　　A. 梨园　　　B. 四川　　　C. 马嵬坡　　D. 长安

11. 杨贵妃死的时候多大年龄?（　　）

　　A. 22 岁　　　B. 28 岁　　　C. 32 岁　　　D. 38 岁

12. 李隆基每天思念杨贵妃,他做了什么?（　　）

　　A. 画了一幅画每天看　　B. 每天看花

　　C. 每天跳舞　　　　　　D. 每天唱歌

13. 高力士找来的道士可以做什么?（　　）

　　A. 唱歌　　　　　　　　B. 跳舞

　　C. 找人的魂魄　　　　　D. 为李隆基的母亲祈福

14. 道士在哪里找到了杨贵妃?（　　）

　　A. 地府　　　B. 月宫　　　C. 马嵬坡　　D. 蓬莱岛

15. 杨贵妃死后去了哪里?（　　）

　　A. 地府　　　　　　　　B. 蓬莱岛

　　C. 天上　　　　　　　　D. 道观

16. 每年的几月几号月宫举行宴会？（　　）

　　A. 一月一日　　　　　B. 三月十五

　　C. 八月十五　　　　　D. 十月十五

17. 谁让李隆基参加月宫的宴会？（　　）

　　A. 玉帝　　B. 杨贵妃　　C. 道士　　D. 杨国忠

18. 在月宫的宴会上，杨贵妃跳的是什么舞？（　　）

　　A. 天宫的舞　　　　　B. 霓裳羽衣舞

　　C. 蓬莱岛的舞　　　　D. 宫殿的舞

19. 杨贵妃在月宫见到李隆基后，她的反应是怎样的？（　　）

　　A. 不认识他　　　　　B. 很高兴

　　C. 不想见他　　　　　D. 没说话就走了

20. 杨贵妃和李隆基永远住在了哪里？（　　）

　　A. 地府　　B. 月宫　　C. 宫殿　　D. 四川

二、判断题：请根据故事内容判断下列说法是否正确，如果正确请标"T"，不正确请标"F"。
Decide whether the following statements are true (T) or false (F).

1. 李隆基最喜欢的妃子病死了之后，他很伤心。　　（　　）

2. 高力士很快就能知道李隆基在想什么。　　　　　（　　）

3. 李隆基带着高力士去四川，见到了杨贵妃。　　　（　　）

4. 李隆基不喜欢看花。（　）

5. 李瑁是李隆基的儿子。（　）

6. 杨玉环是李瑁的好朋友。（　）

7. 杨玉环去道观是因为她不喜欢待在宫殿。（　）

8. 李隆基很喜欢音乐，也喜欢谱曲。（　）

9. 杨贵妃跳舞特别好，所以李隆基给了她金钗。（　）

10. 杨贵妃很喜欢吃荔枝。（　）

11. 荔枝是从北方运来的。（　）

12. 荔枝是用杨贵妃的马运到长安的。（　）

13. 李隆基和杨贵妃感情很好，他们从来不吵架。（　）

14. 杨贵妃经常和她的父亲母亲见面。（　）

15. 专门为杨贵妃做衣服的人有700人。（　）

16. 安史之乱的时候，杨国忠被杀了。（　）

17. 李隆基没想到士兵们会杀了杨国忠。（　）

18. 李隆基和杨贵妃他们到了四川之后，生活很幸福。（　）

19. 李隆基在四川的时候，每天都打仗。（　）

20. 李隆基回到宫殿的时候，十分想念杨贵妃。（　）

三、选择填空。**Choose the appropriate words to fill in the parentheses.**

1. 不久，李隆基（　　）了一个好机会，把杨太真（　　）到皇宫里，（　　）为贵妃，大家都（　　）她杨贵妃。从此以后，杨贵妃和李隆基就（　　）了幸福的生活。

  A. 叫　　　B. 过上　　　C. 找　　　D. 封

  E. 接

2. 李隆基不再是（　　），也不用做管理（　　）的事情，所以他更想杨贵妃了。虽然这个（　　）他的身边还有很多（　　），但是他心里只想着杨贵妃，所以他让人画了一张杨贵妃的（　　）。

  A. 画像　　　B. 皇帝　　　C. 时候　　　D. 妃子

  E. 国家

3. 李隆基正在宫里看着（　　）的时候，（　　）过来了，说："（　　）让我八月十五带您去参加（　　）的（　　），宴会上杨贵妃会跳舞，到时候你们就可以见面了。"

  A. 宴会　　　B. 月宫　　　C. 道士　　　D. 玉帝

  E. 金钗

四、请根据故事内容，按照故事的发展顺序给下列句子排序。（请将句子前的序号填在下面的横线上）
Put the following statements in order according to the story.

杨贵妃的人生经历

成为李隆基儿子李瑁的王妃→_____→去道观为李隆基的母亲祈福→成为李隆基的妃子→_____→李隆基送给她金钗→李隆基为了她能吃到南方的荔枝专门派快马送荔枝→_____→在马嵬坡自杀→_____→在蓬莱岛和道士见面，知道李隆基想她→_____→和李隆基一起在月宫居住

1. 安史之乱发生，和李隆基一起去四川
2. 魂魄去蓬莱岛成为仙女
3. 和李隆基在花园见面
4. 八月十五在月宫和李隆基见面
5. 为《霓裳羽衣曲》配舞

五、连线题。 Match.

1. 选择人物的身份。

   A. 李瑁　　　　　　a. 唐朝的皇帝

   B. 高力士　　　　　b. 最懂皇帝的人

   C. 杨国忠　　　　　c. 杨贵妃以前的名字

   D. 杨玉环　　　　　d. 杨贵妃的哥哥

   E. 李隆基　　　　　e. 李隆基的儿子

2. 根据故事内容为下列事物选择各自的特征。

   A. 荔枝　　　　　　a. 好看的

   B. 金钗　　　　　　b. 好听的

   C. 生活　　　　　　c. 珍贵的

   D. 舞蹈　　　　　　d. 新鲜的

   E. 曲子　　　　　　e. 幸福的

3. 为下列词语选择合适的搭配。

   A. 参加　　　　　　a. 眼泪

   B. 违抗　　　　　　b. 宴会

   C. 承认　　　　　　c. 国家

   D. 管理　　　　　　d. 命令

   E. 流下　　　　　　e. 错误

六、图片题。Answer the following questions according to the picture.

1. 请根据图片说说这幅图应该放在这本书的第（　　　）页。

2. 图片中都有什么人物？

3. 图中的人物在做什么？

4. 他们的心情怎么样？为什么？

5. 请你用中文或英文给这幅图加一个简单的标题说明。

七、思考题。Answer the following questions according to the story.

你觉得李隆基是一个什么样的人？他是一个好皇帝吗？

课后练习题答案 Key to the exercises

一、选择题
1. A   2. D   3. B   4. B   5. C
6. D   7. A   8. C   9. B   10. C
11. D   12. A   13. C   14. D   15. B
16. C   17. A   18. B   19. B   20. B

二、判断题：请根据故事内容判断下列说法是否正确，如果正确请标"T"，不正确请标"F"
1. T   2. T   3. F   4. F   5. T
6. F   7. F   8. T   9. T   10. T
11. F   12. F   13. F   14. F   15. T
16. T   17. T   18. F   19. F   20. T

三、选择填空
1. C   E   D   A   B
2. B   E   C   D   A
3. E   C   D   B   A

四、请根据故事内容，按照故事的发展顺序给下列句子排序
3 → 5 → 1 → 2 → 4

五、连线题
1. A-e B-b C-d D-c E-a
2. A-d B-c C-e D-a E-b
3. A-b B-d C-e D-c E-a

六、图片题
　　（答案略）

七、思考题
　　（答案略）

词汇表
Vocabulary List

保重	v.	bǎozhòng	take care
布	n.	bù	cloth
吵架	v.	chǎojià	have a quarrel
承认	v.	chéngrèn	admit
惩罚	v.	chéngfá	punish
出家	v.	chūjiā	become a monk or nun
戴	v.	dài	wear
挡	v.	dǎng	hide
道观	n.	dàoguàn	Taoist temple
反叛	v.	fǎnpàn	rebel against
妃子	n.	fēizi	concubine
封	v.	fēng	confer (a title) upon
根本	n.	gēnběn	root, essence
孤单	adj.	gūdān	lonely
贵妃	n.	guìfēi	imperial honored consort
跪	v.	guì	kneel
果然	adv.	guǒrán	as expected
皇帝	n.	huángdì	emperor
皇宫	n.	huánggōng	imperial palace
接	v.	jiē	pick up, meet
结束	v.	jiéshù	end
解决	v.	jiějué	resolve
借口	n.	jièkǒu	excuse
金钗	n.	jīnchāi	gold hairpin
久	adj.	jiǔ	for a long time
军队	n.	jūnduì	army
苦	adj.	kǔ	painful, hard
梨树	n.	líshù	pear tree
立刻	adv.	lìkè	immediately
荔枝	n.	lìzhī	lychee
流泪	v.	liúlèi	weep

命令	n.	mìnglìng	command, order
能力	n.	nénglì	capability
叛乱	n.	pànluàn	rebellion, revolt
谱曲	v.	pǔqǔ	compose music
其实	adv.	qíshí	actually
祈福	v.	qífú	pray for blessings
亲人	n.	qīnrén	one's family members
曲子	n.	qǔzi	music
认错	v.	rèncuò	admit mistake
散步	v.	sànbù	take a walk
伤心	adj.	shāngxīn	sad
赏赐	v.	shǎngcì	reward
神仙	n.	shénxiān	immortal
失去	v.	shīqù	lose
诗人	n.	shīrén	poet
试	v.	shì	test, try
首	m.w.	shǒu	piece (often used for songs)
受宠	v.	shòuchǒng	be in sb's favor
书法	n.	shūfǎ	calligraphy
太监	n.	tàijiàn	eunuch
态度	n.	tàidu	attitude
唐朝	n.	Tángcháo	Tang Dynasty
逃	v.	táo	escape
同时	conj.	tóngshí	moreover, in addition
王妃	n.	wángfēi	wife of a prince
王爷	n.	wángye	prince, His Highness
违抗	v.	wéikàng	disobey
无奈	v.	wúnài	have no choice, cannot help but
仙女	n.	xiānnǚ	fairy
消息	n.	xiāoxi	news, information
新鲜	adj.	xīnxian	fresh
兴趣	v.	xìngqù	be interested in
宴会	n.	yànhuì	banquet
意见	n.	yìjiàn	opinion, attitude
着急	v.	zháojí	worry

着迷	*adj.*	zháomí	fascinated, enchanted
珍贵	*adj.*	zhēnguì	precious
真相	*n.*	zhēnxiàng	truth
主动	*adv.*	zhǔdòng	on one's own initiative
祝贺	*v.*	zhùhè	congratulate
抓	*v.*	zhuā	capture
自杀	*v.*	zìshā	kill oneself
尊重	*v.*	zūnzhòng	respect
作为	*v.*	zuòwéi	act as

项目策划：刘小琳　韩　颖
责任编辑：刘小琳　付　眉
英文编辑：吴爱俊
英文审定：黄长奇　James Hutchison
插图绘制：赵倩倩
封面设计：E°T创意工作室

图书在版编目（CIP）数据

四大美女之杨贵妃 / 章辉辉改编 . — 北京：华语教学出版社，2017
（"彩虹桥"汉语分级读物 . 3级：750词）
ISBN 978-7-5138-1324-2

Ⅰ . ①四… Ⅱ . ①章… Ⅲ . ①汉语－对外汉语教学－语言读物 Ⅳ . ① H195.5

中国版本图书馆 CIP 数据核字（2016）第 323008 号

四大美女之杨贵妃

章辉辉　改编
郭　辉　翻译

*

©华语教学出版社有限责任公司
华语教学出版社有限责任公司出版
（中国北京百万庄大街24号　邮政编码 100037）
电话：(86)10-68320585　68997826
传真：(86)10-68997826　68326333
网址：www.sinolingua.com.cn
电子信箱：hyjx@sinolingua.com.cn
新浪微博地址：http://weibo.com/sinolinguavip
北京京华虎彩印刷有限公司印刷
2017年（32开）第 1 版
2017年第 1 版第 1 次印刷
（汉英）
ISBN 978-7-5138-1324-2
定价：19.00元